FINGER KNI

CW00969205

BEGINNERS

A COMPLETE GUIDE TO

KNITTING WITH FINGERS

QUINN PIPER

Table of Contents

CHAPTER ONE

INTRODUCTION

Finger knitting is a fun and clean craft you can analyze in a couple of minutes. All you want to get started is a few yarn and your fingers. It's an incredible craft for children and adults. Even novices could be capable of whip up a easy necklace speedy and without problems. Finger knitting is a first-rate craft for adults, teenagers and youngsters of all ages. If you've ever wanted to learn how to finger knit but didn't know wherein to start this is the location to be. We're going to learn how to solid on, knit rows and cast off. By the stop, you'll be capable of knit a simple garland, necklace or maybe a headband. Finger knitting (occasionally referred to as finger weaving) is a brief and smooth manner to make a simple braid. It's similar to french knitting however an awful lot quicker and doesn't require a knitting dolly. You don't need any fancy substances to get commenced. And really no crochet hooks or knitting needles.

Finger knitting is essentially making a long chain stitch just like in knitting or crochet however instead of a hook or pair of needles, you operate your fingers. I recognise starting a brand new craft can be intimidating so that you could make it as smooth as possible I've protected an clean to grade by grade educational. Finger knitting is a suitable and clean craft for youngsters of every age (from across the a while of five and up, but more youthful kids may be succesful additionally). It's a simple stitch, requires no enjoy or understanding, no system apart from yarn and scissors and it's miles a whole lot, a lot faster and easier than traditional knitting. It's just like french knitting with a comparable result, however quicker and simpler than that too. Finger knitting makes use of loops of yarn slipped over every different to make a woven knit – much like normal knitting. The difference is that you use your palms rather than needles, and, rather than having a couple of stitches on a unmarried unit, like you would with a pair of knitting needles, you've got one stitch on every finger with finger knitting, and you wrap yarn around your hands then slip stitches off in rows – instead of wrapping and slipping every sew in my opinion as you will with knitting needles. Finger knitting makes use of at least one sew and a maximum of four – because you handiest have 4 arms. The thumb isn't used as a needle in finger knitting as the gap among it and the arms would truely reduce to rubble the anxiety. Instead you operate your thumb to secure your yarn when casting on in finger knitting.

CHAPTER TWO

FINGER KNITTING GUIDE FOR BEGINNERS

TOOLS & EQUIPMENT

First, you'll need your materials – yarn and your fingers!

Any type of all-purpose yarn will paintings (even though I have not begun to attempt it with very fine, skinny yarn).

Chunky yarn is incredible for small kids – it's a great deal less complicated to preserve and control. In this academic, I'm the usage of a medium four yarn (I don't 'yarn talk' – that's simply what the package deal says!).

If you're unsure at the excellent yarn to work with look for yarns which can be a 4 (medium) for youngsters and up to 5 (bulky) for adults. This additionally depends on what you need to create but for buying started looking for one of those sorts. If you're buying in man or woman, take the yarn on your hand and region it next on your arms to help you distinguish in case you assume it's miles thick sufficient or too skinny and so forth. Getting the proper length yarn can surely assist you get off at the right foot.

Be conscious that yarn/wool has exceptional terms and size/weight charts within the UK compared to the USA.

• **YARN/WOOL** – this will be pur cotton, polyester or a mix, work with what you can find, have available or what shade your kids just like the most.

• **SCISSORS** – any you need to hand will do

- **STICK/ KNITTING NEEDLE OR CROCHET HOOK** – this is if you want to forestall and feature a break half of manner among your venture. It acts as a marker to prevent your hard paintings from unravelling.

So allow's take a look at the simple steps of finger knitting for beginners.

INSTRUCTIONS

These are commands on how to create a 4 extensive cabel knit fashion. You can use the equal technique to do a single cable knit using 2 hands.

I suggest going for the four finger huge if you are the usage of a thinner wool/yarn so you can gain a wider knit. Also in case you are searching at creating a throw, cushion cowl or ear warmers you might want the broader knit.

STEP ONE

Start by putting the give up of the yarn between your thumb and index finger, retaining it firmly in region. Weave the yarn among your hands going over your index finger, underneath your middle finger, over your ring finger and behind your pinkie. When you move over your index finger this ought to be the pinnacle aspect of your hand in which your knuckles are, then back to loop below your center finger that's your palm facet and so forth. This is what your hand need to appear to be after the first set of loops. Loop the yarn around your pinkie and keep weaving back up in your thumb – this time over your pinkie, below your ring finger, over your middle finger, beneath your index finger bringing the yarn up over the pinnacle of your index finger and laying it across your palm, retaining it in place with your thumb. If you warfare with keeping the tail end taught and out of the manner I determined tucking under a bobble on my wrist helps. This kept it in place however deliver me a bit freedom to transport my hand a bit extra while knitting.

Now you have to have one loop on each finger (see picture below).

Repeat the stairs again, over your index finger, beneath your center finger, etc. At this point you'll have loops on each finger – the tail between your index finger and thumb counts as one loop.

STEP TWO

The subsequent step is to tug the loop closest to your palm up (the bottom loop) and over the outside loop, retaining that second loop for your finger.

Start along with your index finger and flow alongside to your pinkie finger, being cautious.

Loop it over as you probably did the others, moving the tail so it hangs down at the again of your hand and out of the manner.

Now you've got one loop on each finger.

STEP THREE

Begin weaving thru your hands once more (step one) beginning together with your index finger (over index finger, underneath middle finger, over ring finger, beneath pinkie) then wrapping round your pinkie and lower back up until you have got two loops to your hand again.

Repeat step pulling one loop over the other, beginning at the pinkie and working up to the index finger.

Keep repeating those steps till your knitting is as long because it desires to be in your task.

STEP FOUR

When the duration is completed to your pride, it's time to tie it off.

You should have one loop on every finger at this factor. Take the loop off your pinkie and put it on your ring finger. Pull the loop closest on your palm out of your ring finger up and over the loop from your pinkie.

Now repeat – switch the loop out of your ring finger for your center finger, pulling the loop in your middle finger up and over that loop. Transfer the loop out of your middle finger on your index finger and pull the ultimate loop up and over that loop.

At this point, you must have the only last loop. Cut off a brief tail from the stop of the yarn and loop it thru this final loop, tightening it then knotting it off. Do the equal to the alternative cease. Alternatively you could cut a long lenght of yarn and thread it thru each loop to your finger, pull off every loop ensuring the yarn is running thru each one. Pull to convey the thread collectively and tie off on the end growing a knot to hold it from unravelling.

If you were making an infinity headband, you can tie the 2 ends together. But don't do this! We'll be using this finger knitting for novices method to create a few other amusing projects

CHAPTER THREE

HOW TO START FINGER KNITTING

MATERIALS:

- Your selected yarn or wool,

- Your hands.

You can finger knit with anything wool or yarn you've got available but I do propose beginning with a cumbersome yarn like t-shirt yarn. It's satisfactory and chunky which makes it easier to see what you're doing and work with.

I assume once you get going you'll be amazed how quick your chain starts offevolved to form. By the cease of the series, you'll be capable of make a lovely t-blouse yarn braid which could use as a garland, necklace or headscarf.

CASTING ON

1.   Lay your palm flat and going through closer to you. Hold the yarn between your thumb and your index finger.

2.   The tail stop (unfastened end) of your yarn to the left. The

working yarn (nevertheless attached to the ball) to the proper.

3. Weave the running yarn (going from left to right) over your index finger, beneath your middle finger, over your ring finger and behind your little finger.

4. For the following row, take the operating yarn over your little finger, under your ring finger, over your center finger and at the back of your index finger.

Five. Repeat and bring the running yarn around and over your index finger, underneath your middle finger, over your ring finger and in the back of your little finger.

6.   For the very last row, deliver your operating yarn around and over your pinky finger, under your ring finger and over your center finger. Trap the working yarn among your index finger and your middle finger.

7.   Keep the tail cease trapped among your thumb and index finger to forestall it from flying away.

8. With your other hand, pull the lowest row in your pinky finger over the top of your finger. Move in your ring finger and pull the bottom row up over your finger. Repeat to your center finger.

You may need to bend your palms down a chunk as you pull the rows up and over.

9. To finish casting on take the tail (unfastened) give up of the yarn from between your thumb and index finger and bring it ahead.

10. Lift it up and over the yarn between your thumb and index finger. Bring the tail stop at the back of your hand to preserve it out of the way.

THE END

Printed in Great Britain
by Amazon